Original title:
Laurel Laments

Copyright © 2025 Creative Arts Management OÜ
All rights reserved.

Author: Sebastian Whitmore
ISBN HARDBACK: 978-1-80566-737-7
ISBN PAPERBACK: 978-1-80566-866-4

Honor's Hushed Farewell

When leaves took flight, oh what a sight,
They danced around in a merry plight.
A tree sighed deep, with roots to keep,
While whispers of joy played hide and seek.

Brooks giggled low, they knew the show,
As branches bowed in an elegant flow.
One last cringe from the twisting grin,
As nature waved and let chaos in.

Elegy of a Fallen Canopy

Beneath the boughs, where shadows creep,
A squirrel chortles, a secret to keep.
The branches shiver, oh what a quiver,
As acorns drop, their purpose delivered.

A leaf with flair took quite a dare,
It tumbled forth without a care.
The ground was soft, a leafy bed,
As giggles erupted from overhead.

Battle Hymn of the Twisted Branch

Oh twisted branch, you cheeky prank,
With knots and curves, you steal the rank.
While winds be blowin', you shout and ache,
Creating chaos with every shake.

The birds cackle down from above,
Their raucous tunes, a sonnet of love.
While squirrels plot their sneaky raid,
On acorns of fortune your shade has made.

The Lingering Sorrow of Leaves

As twilight drapes its velvet fold,
Leaves reminisce of days of old.
They mumble jokes about the breeze,
And giggle softly as it flees.

From green to gold, their laughter rolled,
Yet still they cling, their hearts so bold.
In whispered tones, they plot a scheme,
To catch the sun in a playful dream.

Serenade of the Sorrowing Crown

With golden leaves that flap about,
A crown that laughs yet wears a pout.
Its branches twist in funny ways,
It chuckles softly through the days.

When breezes blow, it starts to sway,
A jester dressed in green display.
Its sorrow's just a playful jest,
In nature's arms, it finds its rest.

The Weeping Greenery

Oh, how the plants do shed their tears,
With leafy sighs that stir our fears.
Yet in their weeping, joy does bloom,
A forest giggle fills the room.

Each droplet's dance is sheer delight,
A playful prank in morning light.
They smile beneath their tear-stained guise,
A green reprieve, a sweet surprise.

Petals of Nostalgia

Fallen petals tell tales of yore,
Each one a giggle, each one an aww.
They whisper stories to the ground,
In hues of laughter, joy is found.

They scatter memories near and far,
Like jokes exchanged beneath a star.
In every crinkle, life does play,
A comedy of blooms, hooray!

The Unraveling Vine

The vine, it curls, it twists, it twirls,
A dance of green in joyful swirls.
With each unwinding, giggles sprout,
As neighbors watch, they grin and shout.

It trips on stones and tumbles low,
Yet finds its way with graceful flow.
A blurred performance, oh so grand,
Nature's prankster, unplanned, unplanned!

The Script of Leafy Lamentation

When trees have thoughts, oh what a sight,
They giggle leaves like anchors bright.
Though roots feel heavy, trunk stands tall,
They crack jokes at the leaf falls.

Branches sway with playful glee,
Whispering woes of being free.
Yet in their shade, we all can rest,
While nature's puns play out the best.

Through the Veil of Fading Green

In autumn's cloak, the greens do fade,
But leaves find ways to masquerade.
With vibrant costumes, they take a stance,
In a dance of death, they laugh and prance.

The soil chuckles, 'What a scene!'
As leaves become the fallen queen.
They twirl and twist with each strange breeze,
As if to mock the winter's freeze.

Echoes of the Crowned

Oh mighty crown of leafy kings,
Delighted screams of rustling wings.
Each bud a jester, each bloom a jest,
In nature's court, they are the best.

With no regards for hushed lament,
They tickle branches, light and bent.
As sunlight fades and shadows grow,
They grin and giggle, 'We steal the show!'

Whispers of the Wreathed

The wreaths of old, so grandly spun,
Tell tales of laughter, just for fun.
With petals mixed and twigs entwined,
They share the gags that nature's lined.

In every twist, a secret thrives,
Of plant-filled mishaps and merry jives.
In gardens bright, they tease and play,
Their humor blooms, come what may.

A Garland of Forgotten Glories

In the attic of dreams where old trophies lay,
Dust bunnies dance in a whimsical sway.
Tinsel and smiles in a tangled mess,
We wear them like crowns, but who did we bless?

Once bright and bold, now feeling quite shabby,
Our garland of glories is looking quite drabby.
We laugh at the echoes of glory long past,
A tale of a time that just didn't last.

The Mourning Oak

A tree in the park wears a frown so wide,
It lost all its leaves in a comical slide.
With branches like arms, it shakes with despair,
Why must autumn be such a cruel affair?

Squirrels have laughter, they frolic and play,
While Oak thinks of summer, just fading away.
It whispers to passers with a grumpy old croak,
"Join me in mourning," says the weary Oak.

Echoes Beneath the Canopy

Beneath the tall trees where shadows are cast,
Lies a symphony of whispers from ages long past.
The branches sing out, with a giggle and cheer,
While acorns are plotting a prank, I do fear.

"Watch out for the rain!" they mischievously say,
As they drench the poor couple who stroll by today.
A chorus of rustles, a serenade fine,
Leaves chuckle in chaos, "It's all by design!"

Thorns Among the Laurels

Among the sweet laurels, some thorns dare to grow,
With a prick and a poke, they put on a show.
While laurels are chatting, feeling quite grand,
The thorns roll their eyes, forming a band.

They plot little tricks, a mischievous crew,
"Let's turn up the drama, see what we can do!"
As laughter erupts, and the flowers all sway,
In the garden of jest, they all join the fray.

The Emissary of Bitter Fragrance

In the garden, where daisies sway,
A gnarled stem caught in dismay.
Its scent is strong, a scent so bold,
Makes all the bees flee, oh behold!

With every breeze, it starts to brag,
Suggesting others are a drag.
Yet in the soil, it lies alone,
A king with no crown, in flesh and bone.

Weaving Shadows in the Grove

In shadows cast by trees so high,
A squirrel plots, but oh how shy!
It gathers nuts with deft design,
While rolling acorns feel divine.

But watch it leap in awkward flight,
It twirls and tumbles, oh what a sight!
The shadows giggle as they grow,
A dance so silly, it steals the show.

The Gaze of Time Upon the Green

Once a sprout, now a twisty vine,
With dreams of grandeur, oh so fine.
It nods to daisies, full of grace,
Yet whispers, 'Who won this race?'

It ticks and tocks in eloquent blooms,
While grasshoppers plot their tiny dooms.
Time shakes its head, with a sigh or two,
'Oh, growing old is just for you!'

A Tapestry of Wilted Whispers

Leaves chatter softly, gossip in breeze,
'Oh, who's that wilted? It's John with ease!'
They fall and flutter, weaving a tale,
Around the garden, where gossip prevails.

Hardly a rose, just a stem full of woe,
Yet all the flowers want to know:
'How did it happen? Was it the rain?'
And John just sighs, 'Oh, not once again.'

Remnants of Nature's Triumph

In the garden, weeds waltz around,
Claiming their throne, they wear no crown.
Dandelions giggle, they're quite the jest,
While tulips pout, they do their best.

Rabbits hop by, in their tailcoat suits,
Nibbling on carrots, those rooty hoots.
The sunlight chuckles as shadows play,
Nature's comedy, brightening the day.

The Sigh of the Ancients

Once there stood trees, grand and true,
Now they just laugh at the view.
They whisper tales of their distant kin,
But squirrels just scold, 'Where have you been?'

Mossy rocks grumble, covered in green,
Saying, 'We're older than you've ever seen!'
Echoes of time tickle the breeze,
As woodpeckers drum with a spunky tease.

A Fate Adorned in Green

A clump of grass has big dreams to grow,
Yet it's stuck by the fence, feeling quite low.
It eyes the daisies with envy and glee,
'If only I could be as cute as thee!'

The sun beams down, trying to cheer,
But weeds just giggle, 'Oh dear, oh dear!'
Nature's plan is often quite funny,
Who knew plants could have such wit, honey?

Ghosts of the Floral Tides

Petals float by like whispers of old,
Dancing in winds, their stories unfold.
They chuckle at bees, with all of their buzz,
'We're the true stars! Now that's what we was!'

Violets snicker in a violet hue,
'Watch out for roses, they think they're so blue!'
The garden's alive, a comedic parade,
Floral spirits in a leafy charade.

Hushed Cries from the Canopy

In the branches, whispers squeak,
Squirrels chitter, 'What a week!'
Birds are singing off-key tunes,
Even mushrooms are laughing 'neath the moons.

A wise old owl, with glasses cracked,
Sighs for leaves, his dignity hacked.
He tried to pose, but lost his grip,
Fell on a nest, oh what a trip!

Vines wrestle in a tangled show,
Twirling softly, a leafy glow.
The chatter rises with the light,
A verdant party through the night!

Underneath, the roots do snore,
As beetles plot to start a war.
But with a giggle, all is well,
In this tree of tales, we dwell.

Lament of the Verdant Crown

A crown of green with stories worn,
It shudders lightly, forlorn.
The petals weep a gentle haze,
As daisies plan their sunny plays.

The grass sings softly, missing who's gone,
While dandelions puff in quiet con.
They giggle at the clouds that stray,
Turning frowns to cotton candy gray.

A tender breeze, a playful shush,
As willow branches start to blush.
Nights filled with whispers and sighs,
In the verdant crown, laughter flies.

But through it all, a squirrel will prance,
In a comedy show, giving chance.
With every leaf, a chuckle sprigs,
In the midst of green, we do our digs.

A Symphony of Sorrowful Twigs

Twigs in the breeze play a sad refrain,
Bowing low in their leafy pain.
A woodpecker's giggle cracks the night,
As shadows dance in the moonlight.

Branches creak under comedic weight,
Telling tales of an awkward date.
The pinecones drop with a plop and roll,
In a trove of laughter, that is the goal.

The nightingale croons with a wink and nod,
While hedgehogs plot and earthworms prod.
Even the snails with shell-turned humor,
Leave trails of giggles — a slow consumer!

In this raucous dappled flee,
Nature's jokes are plain to see.
Sorrowful twigs, they twist and sway,
In a symphony of funny play.

Wreathed in Memory

Old leaves chuckle in the breeze,
Whispers of past glories tease.
Once adorned with nature's crown,
Now they're just a leafy gown.

The squirrels dance with wild delight,
Poking fun at fading light.
Nostalgia wears a silly hat,
As laughter bounces off the mat.

Dreams of the Withered Vine

Once a vine that climbed so high,
Now it droops and wonders why.
Chasing sunlight, it stumbles down,
Raindrops giggle, wearing frowns.

In a world where blooms are few,
This vine insists it once knew you.
It tells tall tales of summer's heat,
But the garden thinks it's rather sweet.

Golden Promises Lost

The flowers promised gold to me,
But rust has shown their true decree.
Once bright petals, now a gag,
Drifting down, the colors sag.

In a sunbeam, they used to glow,
Now they flail with leaves aglow.
The garden's jesters, oh so spry,
Take a bow as they wave goodbye.

Whispers Among the Twisting Vines

Twisting tales of leafy lore,
Grapes giggle at the garden floor.
They gossip soft, a viney chat,
Where all the critters tip their hat.

Wrapped in stories of the past,
These tangled dreams just might outlast.
With every breeze, a chuckle comes,
As laughter dances with the drums.

Sorrow Among the Petals

In a garden so bright, a bee buzzed by,
Chasing petals that danced, oh my, oh my!
But the flowers just sighed, "Why don't they see?"
Their polka-dot dreams were not meant to be.

With each fluttering leaf, a tale spun anew,
Of roses with thorns, and a tulip or two.
They wished for some laughter, a whimsical jest,
Yet all they got was a bright yellow pest.

Honor's Silent Echo

In the halls of the grand, where statues stand tall,
A squirrel donned armor—he thought he'd have a ball.
But every salute turned into a laugh,
He stumbled and fell, oh what a gaffe!

The echoes of glory turned into a song,
As laughter erupted—this can't be wrong!
With acorns for crowns and a twig for a sword,
The honor was silly, but nobody bored.

Regrets among the Twigs

Beneath a tall oak, a chipmunk did frown,
He buried a nut—right there in the ground.
But come winter's chill, he scratched at the dirt,
"I forgot where I hid it!" Oh, what a hurt!

The clouds rolled like pillows, up high in the sky,
While he danced with regret and let out a cry.
His friends threw a party, with snacks that they found,
"Next time we'll mark it!" They cheered all around.

The Touch of the Green Bough

A branch with a tickle, a leaf with a nudge,
A squirrel squealed softly, but wouldn't quite budge.
"Why's the tree laughing? Is it dizzy with glee?"
As each gentle poke felt like comedy spree.

Those emerald dancers swayed left and right,
While the chipmunks chuckled at this leafy plight.
With whispers of mischief that tickled the air,
They rallied together—no worry, no care.

Shadows in the Glory

In the spotlight, I stumble,
A flower crowned with trouble.
Dancing awkward, I trip and sway,
Who knew grace would run away?

Under branches, whispers tease,
Nature's jokes with playful breeze.
I pose proudly, then I fall,
A bumpy ride? Oh, that's my call!

Proudly adorned, I take my stand,
Searching for my graceful brand.
In this jest, I laugh aloud,
Saplings giggle, nature's crowd!

Twisting vines with joyful flair,
Life's a joke, I must declare.
In glory shrouded, I still cheer,
For laughs abound when friends are near!

A Quiet Anthem for the Honored

Among the blooms, a quiet song,
A nod to those who've bloomed along.
With petals bright and roots so deep,
We celebrate, but oh, we leap!

In jest, our whispers fill the air,
A clumsy waltz without a care.
Each leaf a gentle, winking grin,
To honor those who've been and been!

Together here, we dance the night,
No dignity in sight, just light.
With woven dreams and laughter loud,
We weave our love, a leafy shroud!

So raise a cup to all you see,
The honored ones, let laughter be!
In joy we find our roots entwined,
A silly love, perfectly aligned!

The Green Wreath's Solitude

A garland hangs on an empty chair,
A leafy friend, but no one's there.
Oh solitary, what a show,
The silliest wreath ever to grow!

Birds can laugh from branches high,
At this crown that makes us sigh.
In fancy style, it sits with pride,
But oh, the jest when friends collide!

Who wore this thing, would be the guess,
It seems to yearn for more finesse.
Yet here it stays, a draped delight,
Turning mundane into a fright!

So here's to wreaths of lonely grace,
A funny face in a leafy space.
With smiles and chuckles, it hangs still,
A crown of dreams, and yes, goodwill!

Fragments of Verdant Dreams

In gardens where wild wishes grow,
Silly thoughts begin to flow.
Petals whisper of dreams gone mad,
In fragments bright, a world to add!

With vines that twist and twirl about,
We giggle soft, as joys sprout.
Every leaf a story spun,
Of days gone wild, oh what fun!

Yet somewhere lost, a blossom's hope,
Hiding under a leafy rope.
Each fragment sings, a tune so sweet,
In verdant dreams, life's quite a treat!

To all the petals that bring us cheer,
In laughter's face, we hold them dear.
With every bloom, a belly laugh,
In scenes of green, we find our path!

Cry of the Honored Green

In the garden of greens, I spy some glee,
The shrubs are laughing, as bold as can be.
With every tickle of the breeze so light,
They dance like they're tipsy, what a funny sight!

Oh, the daisies gossip, spilling their cheer,
While the weeds complain, they just want a beer.
A squirrel does ballet, the birds are the band,
In this blighted Eden, life's quite unplanned!

Butterflies flutter in a silly parade,
Chasing their shadows, oh, how they've strayed!
The roses are blushing, they blush just for fun,
Each petal a giggle, in the bright summer sun!

So here's a toast to our whimsical greens,
In laughter and joy, how much fun it seems.
With nature as jest, we find solace in play,
A chuckle or two goes a long, funny way.

The Elegy of Olive Hues

In the olive grove, a sage had a thought,
'Twas not just the fruit, but the laughter it brought.
With olives so round, they bounce like a ball,
Roll down the hill, heed the silly call!

An old tree chuckled, "Young olives, take care,
You'll end up in brine, but do I even dare?"
Each fruit shrieked in horror, then burst out in grins,
Finally accepting, that's where humor begins!

As shadows grew long, the vines waltzed around,
Performing their dance on the lush, hallowed ground.
With jokes to renew, and some tales to spin,
Their laughter echoed, a raucous din!

So gather your olives, toast to good cheer,
Life's just an adventure, let's hold it quite dear.
In the grove's gentle sway, silliness flows,
In hues of bright olives, where laughter still grows.

Shadows on the Path of Victory

The path of success, or so they proclaim,
Is riddled with shadows, but none feel the same.
Like clowns with big shoes, we march that long trail,
In pursuit of the crown, we laugh, and we fail!

Each step is a jig, with hilarity near,
Our triumphs are squeaks, and our failures, great cheer.
The trophies we chase, they wobble and shake,
As we dance through the fog, of the choices we make!

The sun throws its shade, where the jesters convene,
Their antics are wild, but the plot's quite serene.
With whoopee cushions and jokes on a reel,
We conquer the fears, with each funny feel!

So victory's shadow, is laughter in disguise,
Teaching us joy, through the lows and the highs.
A joyous procession, with jesters galore,
On this path of triumph, let laughter restore!

Serpents Among the Foliage

In the underbrush, whispers flicker and slide,
A snake with a hat says, "Come take a ride!"
With a twinkling eye, he juggles some leaves,
Each twist and each turn brings the best of reprieves.

Beneath rolling ferns, the creatures conspire,
To craft a tall tale, that's sure to inspire.
"Why did the snake cross the road?" they all buzz,
"To see if the grass was more green, just because!"

In laughter they slither, with scales oh so bright,
Each coil tells a story, that tickles the night.
They wriggle and giggle, a cheeky parade,
In the follies of nature, their antics won't fade!

So if you should wander where the wild things play,
Expect the gremlins, who'll lead you astray.
With serpents and fables, and pranksters so sly,
In the heart of the foliage, you may laugh and cry!

A Song for Noble Leaves

Once upon a windy day,
Leaves danced in a grand ballet.
They twirled and swirled, oh what a sight,
But some got tangled—what a plight.

With every gust, their dreams took flight,
Some landed soft, others in fright.
A brave little leaf in a silly hat,
Declared, "Look at me! I'm a cool acrobat!"

They laughed and giggled, free and bold,
As summer sun turned into gold.
Yet whispered winds brought tales of doom,
"Next month, you'll all be in the broom!"

So here's to leaves, both grand and small,
Let's raise a cheer, let's have a ball.
For every twist of fate and change,
There's laughter hiding, oh so strange.

Mourning the Leafy Glory

Oh, the mighty branches bend and sway,
Once green and proud, now they decay.
The golden hues seem fine at first,
Yet autumn brings the leaf's own curse.

They reminisced of summer's fun,
Now merely snacks for squirrels on the run.
"Remember the days we'd shimmer and shine?"
"Now we're but crumpled, falling in line!"

A rustling voice said, "Do not fret,
We had our glory, what a set!
Let's make a joke of our sad plight,
I'll rest on your head; what a funny sight!"

So laughter echoed through the trees,
As leaves cherished memories with ease.
In the end, what foil was found?
Beneath our gloom, joy's laughter resounds.

Gilded Grief

In the forest where laughter was rife,
A leaf lamented its former life.
"Once I was fresh, a vibrant green,
Now I'm a crinkle: too sad, too mean."

The others replied with a chuckle or two,
"Your golden glow is quite the view!
You shine like the sun—be proud, dear friend,
Even with a dip, the fun does not end!"

With roots of humor and branches of cheer,
They danced in the breeze, not a single tear.
"Let the winds of fate blow and shriek,
For we're just leaves—no need to be meek!"

So up they twirled, in laughter's embrace,
Finding joy in their leafy disgrace.
For gilded grief can be the belly laugh,
As they jive and spin on nature's path.

The Wreath of Regrets

Oh, come gather 'round, let's have a toast,
To the leaves that swayed and danced the most.
Regrets are heavy, like a lumpy sack,
But who can sigh when we all wear a hat?

So here's the wreath, made from fallen friends,
It's tangled and twisted, but the fun never ends.
With each wilted leaf and every burst,
Let us laugh at the fate that's completely reversed.

A merry band of nature's best,
Each sprinkled chat adds to the jest.
In the circle of fronds, they wink and tease,
"Remember when we thought we were trees?"

So let's bind our woes with a roguish cheer,
For even in sorrow, there's laughter near.
With a twist of fate and a wink of chance,
The wreath of regrets leads to a funny dance.

Ciphers in the Crumpled Leaves

Whispers of secrets in crinkled threads,
Foliage giggles as it jokes 'bout the beds.
Squirrels in tuxedos, dancing around,
Cracking up jokes that are barely profound.

Piles of leaves have a comical drift,
Telling their stories, each one a gift.
A faint rustle mimics a playful cheer,
As autumn chuckles, it's quite the scene here.

Who knew that leaf piles could spark such delight?
Waltzes with wind, twirling in pure flight.
With each tumble and twist, they take their stand,
Nature's own stand-up, a show that is grand.

So gather 'round, all you curious ears,
Listen to foliage banter through years.
With laughter and rustles, they never grow tired,
In the world of the leaves, humor's inspired.

The Language of Twined Stems

Twisted spaghetti of vines in a spree,
Chortling and snickering, oh can't you see?
A tangle of gestures, stems playing coy,
Entwined in a dance, oh what a joy!

Ribbons of green, like gossiping friends,
What stories they tell as the sunlight bends.
Bumblebees buzzing, they can't keep it hush,
Adding to mischief, causing a fuss.

A tickle of petals, a sweep and a dash,
As flowers conspire with a comical flash.
In laughter of nature, they join in the fun,
Entangled in joy 'til the day is done.

So next time you wander where wild things play,
Look closely — hear what the stems have to say.
In the language of vines, joy leaps and churns,
From giggling petals, the laughter returns.

Echoes in the Emerald Silence

In the hush of the wood, with a wink and a sway,
    Trees share their gossip on a sunlit day.
    Echoes of laughter in rustling leaves,
  A melody found where nobody grieves.

  Moss snickers underfoot, soft like a hug,
  While shadows parade with an earnest tug.
  Branches convene, in a high-flying cheer,
Chirping and chuckling to spread the good cheer.

  A breeze that's a tickler blows softly around,
  Causing the branches to dance without sound.
  Nature's own symphony, light and serene,
Plays out amid giggles where silence have been.

So weave through the woods where the beautiful play,
  In the emerald silence, find laughter's bouquet.
    With echoes of humor tickling the air,
  Join the woodland jesters without a care.

Mournful Blooms of Untold Yesterdays

Petals with history, wearing a frown,
Recalling the days when they twirled around.
Stems sighing softly, but look there's a sprout,
Who dances with joy, shaking off all doubt.

With each drooping flower, a wink of the past,
Remembers the sunlight, the good times that passed.
But among all the sighs, there's laughter that's spilled,
A chorus of blooms, the garden is thrilled!

Faded and wrinkled, the blooms still connect,
With cheeky bright daisies that just won't neglect.
So, in the sadness, a humor emerges,
To banish the gloom as their laughter surges.

So lift up your spirits with each gentle sway,
In spite of the shadows, there's joy on display.
For even in sorrow, a giggle can bloom,
In the garden of ages, life bustles and zooms.

Ghosts of the Adorned

Whispers in the garden, dressed in green,
Chasing after dreams that used to glean.
Fairies laugh as they twirl and spin,
While their poltergeist friends bring snacks from the bin.

Banners sway with a ghostly cheer,
What mischief awaits when the night draws near?
Dancing shadows with unmatched flair,
Who's stealing the cake? Oh, do beware!

Frogs in tuxedos croak a tune,
While the sun laughs down, a grumpy moon.
Phantoms juggling apples, what a sight!
Only to trip, oh, what a fright!

But in this realm of ghostly delight,
Laughter echoes through the chilly night.
For even in sorrow, let spirits play,
With memories that twist in a humorous way.

Leaves of Remembrance

Fallen leaves, they tickle the toes,
As stories of old, through the air, do blow.
Squirrels chatter, sharing some glee,
While memories dance under the old oak tree.

Tickling the breeze, they swirl around,
Each leaf a memory, a playful sound.
Pigeons hold court, dressed in fine gray,
Cooing about the antics of yesterday.

As laughter echoes with every gust,
For every leaf's dissolve, there's joy and trust.
A breeze of whispers through branches sways,
As sunlight twinkles in clever ways.

So let's gather laughter, let it take flight,
With leaves that remind us of each silly night.
In this realm of humor, let joy rebound,
For every loss, a chuckle is found.

When the Festival Fades

As night unfolds, the lights grow dim,
A leftover pie sits, looking quite grim.
The jester stumbles, lost in delight,
Tripping over his own joke, oh what a sight!

Confetti drifts like memories past,
While weary revellers long for a blast.
Candles burn low, casting shadows that play,
What happened to laughter? It faded away.

But wait! The music holds a small spark,
A cat with a hat, he starts to embark.
He leads the charge back to the glow,
Where laughter returns, spirits in tow.

So don't let the festival slip into night,
For humor will find us, lingering bright.
In fading moments, joy does invade,
A party's just sleeping, not truly decayed.

Lamenting the Specter of Triumph

A trophy gleams where the dust bunnies play,
Past glories forgotten, they lounge in dismay.
A specter of victory, what a strange sight,
Clinging to whims from long-vanished night.

Sighs from the corners, a ghost on a quest,
To find out what's next in this comical mess.
With trophies a-jiggling, the echoes remain,
Of laughter and pranks that danced in our brain.

Yet here comes a cat, all mischief and cheer,
Flicking trophies like toys, oh dear, oh dear!
For in this old ramble, between joy and strife,
The triumphs remind us of humorous life.

So let's raise a cheer for the spirits so bold,
And remember the times when life made us gold.
In every lament, let us find a new way,
To laugh at the specters of yesterday's play.

Songs for the Fallen Greens

Once a sprightly leaf danced bright,
Now it flops, quite the sight.
Chasing squirrels, it lost the race,
In the wind, it found no grace.

Roots that once held parties grand,
Now just mourn, it's rather bland.
The garden gnomes are shaking heads,
Trading tales of greens that fled.

Whispers of a plant bazaar,
Where all the sprigs have drowned in noir.
Even weeds are off their game,
Stumbling home with leaves of shame.

So here's to quirks in nature's plan,
When even blossoms can't understand.
We laugh at greens that once did strive,
Now they fall, but we survive.

An Ode to Withering Triumph

Oh, the triumphs of the sun,
All the wilting has begun.
Petals droop, a soldier's plight,
Once so bold, now losing light.

With a twist and a grassy cheer,
They've stood their ground, but oh dear!
Now they mutter 'bout the rain,
Wondering if they'll spike again.

Caterpillars laugh with glee,
While the daisies sip their tea.
Victory crowns a stock so frail,
Yet, in jest, they still prevail.

Here's to blooms that fade away,
With humor in disarray.
In fading hues, let's lift a glass,
To all the greens who failed to last.

The Veil of Verdant Sorrow

Once a bush with glossy sheen,
Now a backdrop fit for Halloween.
Shadows whisper of times past,
Where blooms reigned unsurpassed.

Giggles echo through the grass,
As we watch the seedlings pass.
They wear a shroud of leafy green,
Yet, all know what might have been.

The ivy clings with warm embrace,
Yet even it can't keep the pace.
Puddles laugh with bitter tears,
Gardens echo ancient fears.

So let's toast to verdant woes,
And dance in shoes of compost throws.
For every leaf that withers down,
We'll wear our laughter like a crown.

Curses in the Canopy

High above in branches grand,
A squirrel plops, oh what a plan!
Sprightly nuts swing from a bough,
Only to crash—was that a cow?

Twisted twigs hold secrets old,
Lemons sulk, their stories told.
Trees throw shade with grumbling sounds,
As weeds chime in with hasty rounds.

A canopy of sighs and sweets,
Jeers of petals facing defeats.
Yet amidst the leafy gloom,
Laughter wafts, there's still some room.

So lift a cup to all that falls,
To nature's quirks within these walls.
In curses soft and chuckles loud,
We'll cheer for greens, our humor proud.

The Gentle Crumbling of Glory

A crown sits high, but slips with grace,
Leaves fall like jokes in a crowded space.
Once I was grand, now I'm a snack,
Biting on moments I can't get back.

Pomp and pride, they rolled on by,
Now I just laugh and wonder why.
With every chuckle, more dust does collect,
Funny how glory's an old speck.

In the garden, I tell my tales,
To bugs and blooms with curious scales.
Witty quips I share with the breeze,
Who knew my end would make such a tease?

Yet in this crumble, I find my jest,
Even in falling, I feel truly blessed.
A comedian's heart in a wilted show,
At least I'm the star of this funny glow.

A Crown of Shadows

Through shadows cast by a jester's flair,
A crown of mischief floats in the air.
Every wiggle and giggle that treads,
Tells a story with humorous threads.

Once a symbol of elegant grace,
Now I wear humor like a new face.
The past glimmers with a wink and a nod,
As laughter dances where the shadows trod.

In the hall of echoes, my tales abound,
With every punchline, I spin round and round.
Here's to the misfits and fun-loving wits,
We're the glories the world never quits.

So let the darkness play its grand part,
In the spotlight of laughter, we make our start.
For in every shadow, a chuckle we find,
A crown of shadows with a heart so kind.

Reflections in the Green

In emerald fields where I prance and pose,
Whispers of giggles tickle my toes.
Reflections of glory sway with the breeze,
Dancing with shades of humorous tease.

I peek at the puddles where laughter will flow,
Chasing my shadows, putting on a show.
Who knew the grass could sprout such delight,
While dimming the glories that soared in bright light?

Every leaf a mirthful grin,
Telling tales of the glory within.
I tickle the ferns and twirl with delight,
As nature's own stand-up takes flight tonight.

So join in the fun of this green parade,
Where giggles and glory will never fade.
Let's toast to the laughs and the bright, funny sheen,
In the world of reflections, forever we glean.

The Sighing Grove

In a grove where giggles blend with the sighs,
Oh, how the branches roll their eyes!
Once lofty, now playful in humble repose,
Nature's own jesters can give you a doze.

A moan from the bark, a chuckle from leaves,
Tales of the glory that no one believes.
Rustling with laughter, they sway to the tune,
Sipping on sunlight beneath the round moon.

In the shade, I sit and bask in the cheer,
Old stories that tickle the ear.
The jokes we share in this funny retreat,
Make the sighing grove feel whole and complete.

So let's raise a glass to the grove's merry play,
Where humor and sighs blend joy in their sway.
In this gentle space, we find our resolve,
As the crown of the grove starts to evolve.

When Triumph Turns to Twilight

In battle's flair, I danced with glee,
But tripped on pride, oh woe is me!
The crowd erupted, laughter so bright,
As I tumbled down, a glorious sight.

Yet in the chaos, smiles did bloom,
My mighty fall filled the air with Zoom!
As cheers turned to chuckles, fate took a bow,
And I learned that glory can flip, somehow.

I wielded dreams like swords of might,
But forgot to check if my shoes were right.
With every slip, I found my grace,
In funny falls, I found my place.

So here's to triumphs that twist and twirl,
To laugh at life, let laughter unfurl!
Some fights are won with a slip or trip,
A dance of folly, oh what a trip!

The Quiet Boughs Weep

Beneath the trees, I stole a glance,
At boughs that swayed, in a gentle dance.
They whispered tales of days gone by,
While I just laughed, "Don't be so shy!"

The branches drooped, in solemn tune,
As squirrels plotted their heist by noon.
I told them jokes, they rustled leaves,
Yet still, they sighed, as if in thieves.

"Oh lighten up!" I called out loud,
"You wear those frowns like a fluffy cloud!"
But shadows lingered in their show,
I grinned, "Let's play, let's steal the glow!"

So under the weeping, funny trees,
We spun our laughter into the breeze.
With every chuckle, the sunlight leaped,
And even boughs of sorrow, sweetly weeped.

Wreaths of Wistfulness

In gardens rich with tangled vines,
I wove a crown of silly signs.
But every flower had a quirk,
With petals giggling, oh what a perk!

The daisies dared to tease my hair,
The roses blushed, as if in despair.
Yet lilies laughed, their humor spry,
"Wear us proudly! We're not that shy!"

As I adorned my head with glee,
The flowers' chuckles rang like glee.
I danced through fields, a sight so rare,
With wreaths of humor upon my hair.

For life's a jest, a jolly game,
With blooms and jokes that bear no shame.
So wear your wreaths, let laughter soar,
And in your heart, keep wanting more!

The Fallen Heroes' Murmurs

In shadows cast by past estates,
I heard the whispers of silly fates.
The fallen heroes rolled their eyes,
"Why'd we wear tights? Oh what a surprise!"

They rallied forth in dreams of cheer,
Yet tripped on capes, it was all too clear.
With battle cries that turned to snorts,
Their gallant quests were just oldorts!

One claimed his sword was just a prop,
Another yelled, "Hey, watch me hop!"
In every tale, a giggle shone,
As legends laughed in their funny zone.

So raise a glass to those who fell,
And let their stories make you yell!
For even heroes with capes askew,
Know laughter's the mightiest, oh that's true!

The Bitter Sweetness of Glory

In the garden where winners play,
A trophy fell, it rolled away.
Laughing harder than we should,
Lamenting champs, misunderstood.

With each victory, a slice of pie,
Calories etched in the sky.
Rich flavors drown our humble fates,
As we crown our dubious mates.

The medals clink like old church bells,
While friends recount our epic fails.
Take a bow, rejoice through tears,
For glory's sweet taste lasts for years.

So here we dance, the winners lost,
With chuckles echoing at our cost.
In laughter's arms, the loss is bright,
Till dawn breaks in with morning light.

Leaves of Longing

In autumn's breeze, we crave some cheer,
Finding laughter in fallen tears.
Leaves twist 'round like waltzing mice,
Longing for warmth, they pay the price.

Each rustling leaf tells a joke or two,
About dreams that never came true.
We share a grin with the golden trees,
As branches wave in the playful breeze.

With every crunch beneath our feet,
Life's funny quirks can't be beat.
Like squirrels in search of their acorns,
We scavenge joy from life's stirrings.

So dance with us through this fleeting art,
As laughter fills the autumn heart.
In leaves of longing, lives entwine,
Creating stories, oh so divine.

The Crown of Forgotten Eulogies

Amidst the ashes of long-lost dreams,
We wear our crowns, yet nothing gleams.
Echoes of laughter fill the air,
While we pretend we don't care.

Monuments of misplaced praise,
Keep memories wrapped in a daze.
Forgotten tales of glory days,
In eulogies wrapped with funny ways.

The whispers of laughter haunt our halls,
Cracking jokes in shadowed walls.
Like jesters witfully draped in rue,
We conduct a dance that feels brand new.

So here's to crowns of laughter's lore,
As we toast to future and more.
With humor bright amidst the gloom,
In laughter's light, our spirits bloom.

Ghosts of the Green

In the fields where spirits roam,
Golfing ghosts call this place home.
They swing their clubs with laughter bold,
As stories of their strokes unfold.

Each ball they lost, a tale to tell,
With echoes ringing like a bell.
Greens that sigh from endless play,
Haunt our games in a funny way.

With forks and spoons, they serve their tea,
Chortling softly, just like me.
In birdies missed and putts gone wrong,
We find the rhythm of the song.

So here's to spirits on the green,
With antics lively and unseen.
A round of laughs in fading light,
We play with ghosts till the stars shine bright.

The Crown of Glistening Tears

In a garden where giggles grow,
Petals dance in a silly row.
Crowned by droplets, dewdrops gleam,
A clownish plant, it seems to dream.

With butterflies wearing goofy hats,
And grasshoppers telling tales of rats.
Each tear a laugh, a whimsy sprout,
In this crown, all worries pout.

Beneath the sun, the flowers prance,
Spinning round in a wobbly dance.
A bumblebee with a lopsided buzz,
Makes all the blunders feel like a buzz.

So come and share this jolly sight,
Where joy is found in morning light.
With every tear, let laughter flow,
In a world where silliness steals the show.

Tales from the Hollow Bower

In a bower where whispers play,
Squirrels converse in a nutty way.
Tales of mishaps and feathery flights,
All wrapped in laughter, under starry nights.

A raccoon dreams of a pizza feast,
And a shy little rabbit turns into a beast.
With every thump and every hop,
The woodland giggles, can't ever stop.

Eavesdropping elves with wiggly ears,
Curious about the silly ideas.
They chuckle loudly, sharing the lore,
Of a frog who thought he could soar.

In this hollow, where mischief brews,
Every creature sports mismatched shoes.
A tapestry woven of laughter and cheer,
Where stories keep the spirits near.

Memory of the Woven Twigs

In a nest of wobbly wires and twigs,
Sits an owl that knows all the jigs.
She tells of the time a squirrel slipped by,
And ended up with a pie in the sky.

With each wet twig, a memory shines,
Of cheeky raccoons and their hasty designs.
A tapestry stitched with giggles so bright,
Echoes of laughter in the cool night.

Each weave holds a tale of stumbles and falls,
Of a bear who danced in oversized halls.
Remembering moments, zany and fine,
In the confines of her crafty twine.

So pause for a minute, take in the view,
Where memories blend and laughter renews.
In a world made of humor, twigs, and dreams,
Life is sweeter than it seems.

Fading Glory on the Forest Floor

In shadows, where whispers hide,
Mushrooms dance, they're filled with pride.
Holding court in a dappled light,
With snickers shared as day turns to night.

Dead leaves chuckle, giving way,
To cheeky ferns that want to stay.
Each crunch underfoot, a playful tease,
That brings forth giggles in the autumn breeze.

A majestic trunk with bark that's cracked,
Holds tales of glory, sweetly stacked.
Yet here on the floor, the laughter's loud,
As critters gather, fun wrapped in a shroud.

So let's rejoice in this fading grace,
Where every creature finds its place.
In the forest's heart, let's laugh some more,
And celebrate what life has in store.

Shadows Beneath the Canopy

In the shade where the green leaves sway,
The squirrels gossip of the day.
They chat about the lost acorn prize,
While dancing 'neath the laughing skies.

The breeze tickles the branches high,
The flowers giggle, 'Oh my, oh my!'
With sunshine jokes that tickle the ground,
And little creatures just laugh around.

A shadow sneezes, a branch does creak,
The whole forest bursts out in cheek.
Who knew nature had such a flair,
For playful banter floating in air?

So next time you're lost in nature's seat,
Remember the whimsy and join the beat.
Let shadows dance on a joyful spree,
As laughter blooms eternally free.

When Petals Fall from Grace

A petal slipped on its royal sail,
Decided to tell a silly tale.
It fluttered down with a comic twist,
Landing right on a bee's fuzzy fist.

The flowers giggled, 'Oh look, oh dear!'
As the bee buzzed back, 'Not that, my dear!'
The bloom blushed bright, it couldn't deny,
That falling can be quite the sly spy.

Once a rose, it felt so grand,
Now in the dirt, it can't understand.
But laughter is bright in the garden's face,
Even flowers can stumble with grace.

So when petals tumble and start to roll,
Remember they're just playing their role.
They may fall, yet there's never a waste,
In the whimsical dance they embrace.

The Crown's Silent Grief

A crown upon a flower's head,
Sighed softly, 'I feel misled!'
With leaves like jewels, it thought it neat,
But oh, the weight was such a feat!

It longed for breezes, to dance away,
Instead, it awkwardly began to sway.
The winds just chuckled, teased with a jest,
While petals flopped—oh, so unpressed!

Complaints of beauty echoed through the bloom,
As insects giggled, their merriment zoomed.
"Why wear a crown that you can't keep?"
A grasshopper said, "You're just a creep!"

But in the light of the laughing sun,
The crown found joy in every pun.
For even a flower can learn to be free,
In the garden's theater of comedy.

Tales of the Worn Branches

The branches creaked with ancient jokes,
Whispering tales of the silly folks.
Once stood proud, now quite bent,
Sharing secrets of time well spent.

The woodpecker chimed in with a rap,
While robins giggled all around the map.
"It's not the age, but the tales you spin,
That makes us grin, let the fun begin!"

With leaves that rustle like towels on stretch,
They all laughed hard, without a sketch.
For wisdom is funny, as all can see,
Even gnarled branches love comedy.

So next time you wander through woods so grand,
Eavesdrop on stories, take a stand.
For nature's humor is rich and vast,
In every twig, a smile is cast.

www.ingramcontent.com/pod-product-compliance
Lightning Source LLC
Chambersburg PA
CBHW071821160426
43209CB00003B/155